COOKING
FOR 1 OR 2

LAKELAND

Lakeland and Bauer Media Ltd hereby exclude all liability to the extent permitted by law for any errors or omission in this book and for any loss, damage or expense (whether direct or indirect) suffered by a third party relying on any information contained in this book.

This book was created in 2013 for Lakeland by AWW Books, an imprint of Octopus Publishing Group Ltd, based on materials licensed to it by Bauer Media Books, Sydney.

Bauer Media Limited
54 Park St, Sydney
GPO Box 4088, Sydney, NSW 2001
www.awwcookbooks.com.au

 BAUER
MEDIA GROUP

OCTOPUS PUBLISHING GROUP
Design – Chris Bell
Food Director – Pamela Clark

Published for Lakeland in the United Kingdom by Octopus Publishing Group Limited

Endeavour House
189 Shaftesbury Avenue
London WC2H 8JY
United Kingdom
phone + 44 (0) 207 632 5400;
fax + 44 (0) 207 632 5405
aww@octopusbooks.co.uk;
www.octopusbooks.co.uk
www.australian-womens-weekly.com

Printed and bound in China

A catalogue record for this book is available from the British Library.

ISBN 978-1-909770-04-1

© Bauer Media Limited 2013
ABN 18 053 273 546
This publication is copyright. No part of it may be reproduced or transmitted in any form without the written permission of the Publisher.

The Department of Health advises that eggs should not be consumed raw. This book contains some dishes made with raw or lightly cooked eggs. It is prudent for vulnerable people such as pregnant and nursing mothers, invalids, the elderly, babies and young children to avoid uncooked or lightly cooked dishes made with eggs. Once prepared, these dishes should be kept refrigerated and used promptly.

This book also includes dishes made with nuts and nut derivatives. It is advisable for those with known allergic reactions to nuts and nut derivatives and those who may be potentially vulnerable to these allergies, such as pregnant and nursing mothers, invalids, the elderly, babies and children to avoid dishes made with nuts and nut oils. It is also prudent to check the labels of pre-prepared ingredients for the possible inclusion of nut derivatives.

Some of the recipes in this book have appeared in other publications.

COOKING
FOR 1 OR 2

Cooking for just one or two doesn't mean having to settle for cheese on toast or a can of soup. In this collection of 56 delicious recipes you will find snacks and lunchtime choices, simple yet satisfying midweek suppers, and impressive starters, main courses and desserts for special occasions plus a handy chapter of recipes to make now and freeze for later.

One of an exciting new series of cookbooks from Lakeland, *Cooking for 1 or 2* is packed with delicious colour photos plus expert hints, tips and techniques for beginners and experienced cooks alike.

With every recipe triple-tested® for perfect results, these excellent cookbooks are sure to be some of the best-loved on your kitchen bookshelf. To discover the rest of the range, together with our unrivalled selection of creative kitchenware, visit one of our friendly Lakeland stores or shop online at www.lakeland.co.uk.

CONTENTS

A TABLE FOR ONE OR TWO 6

SNACKS & LUNCHES 8

MIDWEEK SUPPERS 32

SOMETHING SPECIAL 60

COOK & FREEZE 84

DESSERTS 100

GLOSSARY 124

INDEX 126

CONVERSION CHARTS 128

A TABLE FOR ONE OR TWO

When eating alone or cooking for just two, it can be tempting simply to open a can of soup or settle for takeaways. But you'll be missing out on so much if you do. There are lots of pleasures to be had in cooking for one or two people.

It is important for us all to eat a variety of healthy delicious food, so experiment to avoid monotony. Don't be afraid to try new combinations of food – one of the great benefits of cooking for yourself is that you don't have to try to please lots of other people; you can cook using the food and the combinations of ingredients that you enjoy.

SHOPPING

It is often more economical to buy large quantities of meat, fish and poultry. Divide it into portions, then wrap, label and freeze them. You can apply this to other foods too: divide a big bag of frozen vegetables and package them in zip-lock freezer bags, wrap and freeze a couple of bacon rashers or sausages in pairs.

It's a good idea to buy smaller quantities of more kinds of fresh fruit and vegetables. That way there is less waste, as you won't need throw out spoiled fruit and veg that you haven't managed to eat, and you get a lot more variety. To ring the changes even more, you could aim to add a vegetable you don't often cook or an exotic fruit you've never eaten to your shopping basket each week.

Think about complementary recipes so, if you need only half a jar or packet of a particular ingredient for one recipe, aim to use the rest in another recipe, so that there is no waste.

Browse the ethnic food aisle of your supermarket or make a visit to an Asian or Middle Eastern food shop and discover brand new worlds of flavours and ideas. Use exotic seasonings to add flair to some of your more basic recipes.

Most bottles and jars can be covered and stored in the refrigerator if you don't use all their contents. Repackage food that comes in cans or plastic containers into glass.

Ultra-healthy eggs naturally come in one-person servings and are endlessly versatile, so keep some to hand in your kitchen for omelettes, frittatas, simple scrambled or baked eggs and more.

COOK ONCE AND EAT TWICE

Save time and think ahead to those times when you're too tired or rushed to cook by preparing larger meals and freezing single or double portions to eat another time. Soups, curries and stews generally freeze well and improve in flavour. The Cook & Freeze chapter in this book (see page 84) has some delicious recipes to choose from.

Get creative with leftovers too. If you don't want to eat the same meal twice in a row, having leftovers is a great starting place for other meals. Use leftover grilled chicken from tonight's supper for tomorrow's chicken and salad sandwiches or combined with salsa and avocado in a tortilla wrap, for example, or use cold rice as the basis of a rice salad.

SNACKS & LUNCHES

HAM, BRIE & FIG SALAD

50g radicchio lettuce leaves
20g rocket
100g thinly sliced ham
1 medium fig (60g), quartered
40g blue brie cheese, sliced thinly

honey mustard dressing
1 teaspoon wholegrain mustard
½ teaspoon honey
1 tablespoon olive oil
1 tablespoon lemon juice

1 To make the honey mustard dressing, place ingredients in screw-top jar; shake well.
2 Arrange lettuce, rocket, ham, fig and cheese on serving plate; drizzle with dressing.

prep time 10 minutes
serves 1
nutritional count per serving
36.2g total fat (12.1g saturated fat); 1998kJ (478 cal); 9g carbohydrate; 28.3g protein; 2.7g fibre

FETA DIP WITH ASPARAGUS, RADISHES & BEANS

250g Greek-style yogurt
100g feta cheese, chopped finely
1 tablespoon coarsely chopped fresh mint
1 tablespoon finely chopped fresh oregano
200g asparagus, trimmed
100g fine green beans, trimmed
4 radishes (140g), trimmed

1 Combine yogurt, cheese and herbs in medium bowl.
2 Add asparagus and beans to frying pan of boiling water; return to a boil, then drain immediately.
3 Place asparagus and beans in bowl of iced water until cold; drain well.
4 Serve dip with asparagus, beans and radishes or, if desired, bread and crackers.

prep + cook time 20 minutes
serves 2
nutritional count per serving
20.8g total fat (13.4g saturated fat); 1409kJ (337 cal); 15.4g carbohydrate; 20g protein; 3.8g fibre

CROQUE-MONSIEUR

4 slices wholemeal bread
90g thinly sliced ham
20g butter

cheese sauce
10g butter
2 teaspoons plain flour
5 tablespoons milk
40g cheddar cheese, coarsely
  grated
2 teaspoons finely chopped fresh
  flat-leaf parsley

1 To make cheese sauce, melt butter in small saucepan, add flour; cook, stirring, until mixture bubbles and thickens. Gradually add milk; cook, stirring, until sauce boils and thickens. Remove from heat; stir in cheese and parsley.
2 Spread sauce on two slices of bread; top two slices with ham then top with remaining bread.
3 Melt remaining 20g butter in large frying pan. Add sandwiches; cook, until browned both sides. Cut into triangles to serve.

prep + cook time 25 minutes
serves 2
nutritional count per sandwich
25.9g total fat (15g saturated fat); 2077kJ (497 cal); 38.4g carbohydrate; 24.8g protein; 5.8g fibre

WRAPS FOUR WAYS

PASTRAMI & CHEESE WRAP

Place 2 thin tortilla wraps together, spread with a rounded tablespoon of tomato chutney. Top with 15g baby spinach leaves, 60g coarsely grated cheddar cheese and 75g wafer-thin pastrami or ham; roll to enclose. Repeat with tortilla wraps, tomato chutney, spinach, cheese and pastrami to make another wrap. Cut wraps into thirds crossways to serve.

prep + cook time 15 minutes
serves 2
nutritional count per wrap 9.2g total fat (5.2g saturated fat); 782kJ (187 cal); 13.9g carbohydrate; 11.7g protein; 1.2g fibre

TURKEY & CRANBERRY WRAP

Spread 2 thin wholemeal tortilla wraps evenly with 2 tablespoons cranberry sauce; top with 80g wafer-thin turkey, 30g trimmed pea shoots and 30g baby spinach leaves. Roll to enclose.

prep + cook time 5 minutes
serves 2
nutritional count per serving 2.1g total fat (0.4g saturated fat); 849kJ (203 cal); 27.6g carbohydrate; 16.7g protein; 2.5g fibre

RICOTTA, BASIL & HAM WRAP

Preheat sandwich press. Slice 2 small courgettes lengthways into ribbons using a vegetable peeler. Divide 60g ricotta cheese among 2 thin tortilla wraps; top with courgettes, 75g wafer-thin ham and 3 tablespoons coarsely chopped fresh basil. Roll to enclose. Toast wraps in sandwich press for about 3 minutes; cut in half to serve.

prep + cook time 8 minutes
serves 2
nutritional count per serving 4.7g total fat (2.3g saturated fat); 886kJ (212 cal); 24.1g carbohydrate; 16.1g protein; 3.7g fibre

DIJON CHICKEN & SALAD WRAP

Spray 200g chicken breast fillets with cooking oil; cook chicken in heated small frying pan. Cool; shred coarsely. Combine chicken in medium bowl with 1 tablespoon fat-free natural yogurt and 1 teaspoon dijon mustard. Divide chicken mixture between 2 thin wholemeal tortilla wraps; top with 30g baby spinach leaves, 1 thinly sliced small tomato and 1 coarsely grated small carrot. Roll to enclose filling.

prep + cook time 25 minutes
serves 2
nutritional count per serving 3.8g total fat (0.7g saturated fat); 932kJ (223 cal); 17.9g carbohydrate; 27.4g protein; 3.2g fibre

CREAMY CHICKEN & PASTA SALAD

375ml water
200g chicken breast fillets
250g large pasta shells
1 celery stalk (150g), trimmed,
  sliced thinly
1 small red onion (100g), sliced
  thinly
60g pecans, toasted
45g thinly sliced pickled dill
  cucumbers
30g rocket leaves

creamy tarragon dressing
100g mayonnaise
60g soured cream
1 tablespoon lemon juice
2 teaspoons finely chopped fresh
  tarragon

1 Bring the water to the boil in small saucepan, add chicken; simmer, covered, about 10 minutes. Cool chicken in poaching liquid 10 minutes; drain, slice thinly.
2 Meanwhile, cook pasta in large saucepan of boiling water until tender; drain. Rinse under cold water; drain.
3 To make creamy tarragon dressing, combine ingredients in small bowl.
4 Combine pasta in large bowl with chicken, dressing and remaining ingredients.

prep + cook time 35 minutes
serves 2
nutritional count per serving
39.1g total fat (8.8g saturated fat); 3097kJ (741 cal); 67.5g carbohydrate; 27.1g protein; 5.7g fibre

BEETROOT, ASPARAGUS & FETA SALAD

100g asparagus, halved
50g feta cheese, crumbled
3 tablespoons torn fresh mint
  leaves
100g cooked beetroot, quartered
2 tablespoons walnut halves,
  toasted

lemon dressing
1 clove garlic, crushed
1 tablespoon olive oil
2 teaspoons lemon juice

1 To make lemon dressing, combine ingredients in small jug.
2 Boil, steam or microwave asparagus until just tender; drain.
3 Combine asparagus, cheese, mint, beetroot, nuts and dressing in medium bowl.

prep + cook time 15 minutes
serves 1
nutritional count per serving
42.7g total fat (11.1g saturated fat); 2052kJ (491 cal); 9.5g carbohydrate; 15.6g protein; 5.8g fibre

EGG & BACON SALAD

1 small sweet potato (250g), cut
  into 2.5cm pieces
cooking oil spray
2 rindless bacon slices (130g)
3 hard-boiled eggs, quartered
½ stalk celery (75g), trimmed,
  sliced thinly
40g mixed salad leaves

honey mustard dressing
75g mayonnaise
1½ tablespoons cider vinegar
2 teaspoons honey
1 teaspoon wholegrain mustard

1 Preheat oven to 220°C/200°C
fan-assisted.
2 Place sweet potato on oven
tray; spray with cooking oil. Roast,
uncovered, about 20 minutes or
until tender.
3 Meanwhile, cook bacon in
heated medium frying pan;
drain on absorbent paper. Chop
coarsely.
4 To make honey mustard
dressing, combine ingredients
in small bowl.
5 Combine sweet potato,
bacon, dressing and remaining
ingredients in large bowl.

prep + cook time 25 minutes
serves 2
nutritional count per serving
29.2g total fat (6.9g saturated
fat); 1965kJ (470 cal); 25.9g
carbohydrate; 25g protein;
2.6g fibre

PORK & CHEESE QUESADILLAS WITH GUACAMOLE

2 teaspoons olive oil

250g minced pork

1 small green pepper (150g), chopped finely

1 fresh long red chilli, chopped finely

1 clove garlic, crushed

3 tablespoons coarsely chopped fresh coriander

4 tortilla wraps

1 tablespoon olive oil, extra

125g grated cheddar cheese

guacamole

1 large avocado (320g), chopped coarsely

½ small plum tomato (45g), deseeded, chopped finely

½ small red onion (50g), chopped finely

½ fresh long red chilli, chopped finely

2 tablespoons finely chopped fresh coriander

1 tablespoon lime juice

1 Heat oil in medium frying pan; cook pork, stirring, about 10 minutes or until browned. Add pepper, chilli and garlic; cook, stirring, until fragrant. Remove from heat, stir in coriander.

2 To make guacamole, place avocado in small bowl; mash roughly with fork. Add remaining ingredients; stir until combined.

3 Brush one side of the tortillas with the extra oil. Turn two tortillas oiled-side down; spread evenly with pork mixture, sprinkle with cheese. Top with remaining tortillas, oiled side up.

4 Cook tortillas, in batches, in heated sandwich press or large frying pan until browned lightly.

5 Cut quesadillas into quarters; serve with guacamole.

prep + cook time 50 minutes
serves 2
nutritional count per serving
75.5g total fat (25.1g saturated fat); 4627kJ (1107 cal); 52.3g carbohydrate; 52.6g protein; 5.9g fibre

MINI BAKED RICOTTA WITH ROAST VEGETABLES

250g ricotta cheese
20g finely grated parmesan
   cheese
1 egg
2 tablespoons finely chopped
   fresh oregano
1 teaspoon finely grated lemon
   rind
½ fresh long red chilli, chopped
   finely
2 baby aubergines (120g),
   quartered
200g baby carrots, trimmed
1 small red pepper (150g), sliced
   thickly
1 tablespoon lemon juice
1 teaspoon olive oil
1 teaspoon fresh oregano leaves

1 Preheat oven to 220°C/200°C fan-assisted. Oil two holes of 6-hole (180ml) large muffin tin.
2 Combine cheeses, egg, oregano, rind and chilli in medium bowl; divide mixture among muffin tin holes. Bake, uncovered, about 20 minutes or until browned lightly and firm.
3 Meanwhile, combine aubergine, carrots, pepper, juice and oil in medium oiled shallow baking dish; roast, uncovered, 20 minutes or until tender. Sprinkle ricotta with oregano leaves; serve with vegetables.

prep + cook time 30 minutes
serves 2
nutritional count per serving
21.7g total fat (10.5g saturated fat); 1438kJ (344 cal); 12.3g carbohydrate; 22.7g protein; 5.2g fibre

GRIDDLED VEGETABLES & HALOUMI WITH LEMON BASIL DRESSING

50g baby spinach leaves
50g char-grilled red pepper,
    sliced thickly
50g marinated artichokes, halved
2 tablespoons green olives
1 portobello mushroom
10g haloumi cheese, sliced thickly

lemon basil dressing
2 teaspoons lemon juice
1 tablespoon extra virgin olive oil
1 tablespoon finely shredded
    fresh basil

1 Combine spinach, pepper, artichoke and olives in large bowl.
2 Place ingredients for lemon basil dressing in screw-top jar; shake well.
3 Cook mushroom on heated, oiled griddle pan, loosely covered with foil, about 5 minutes or until browned and tender, cover to keep warm.
4 Cook cheese, in batches, on griddle pan until browned lightly both sides.
5 Top spinach mixture with mushroom, cheese and dressing.

prep + cook time 20 minutes
serves 1
nutritional count per serving
25.8g total fat (4.4g saturated fat); 1195kJ (286 cal); 5.4g carbohydrate; 6.4g protein; 3.2g fibre

FREE-FORM CARAMELISED LEEK TARTS

1 tablespoon olive oil

1 medium brown onion (150g), sliced thinly

1 medium leek (350g), trimmed, sliced thinly

2 teaspoons fresh thyme leaves

240g ricotta cheese

2 tablespoons coarsely grated parmesan cheese

1 egg, separated

2 sheets ready-rolled shortcrust pastry (appx. 230g each)

1 Heat oil in medium frying pan; cook onion and leek, stirring, about 15 minutes or until mixture starts to caramelise. Stir in thyme; cool.

2 Meanwhile, combine ricotta, parmesan and egg yolk in small bowl.

3 Preheat oven to 200°C/180°C fan-assisted. Oil an oven tray; line with baking parchment.

4 Using 20cm plate as a guide, cut 1 round from each pastry sheet; place rounds on tray. Divide ricotta mixture between rounds, leaving 4cm border around edges.

5 Divide leek mixture over rounds. Turn border of each tart up around filling; brush upturned edges with egg white. Bake about 35 minutes or until pastry is browned lightly.

prep + cook time 1 hour 20 minutes
serves 2
nutritional count per serving
70g total fat (34.3g saturated fat); 4531kJ (1084 cal); 83.2g carbohydrate; 28.3g protein; 7.1g fibre

MIDWEEK
SUPPERS

HERBED CHICKEN SCHNITZEL

2 chicken breast fillets (400g)
2 tablespoons plain flour
1 egg
1 tablespoon milk
85g stale white breadcrumbs
1 teaspoon finely grated lemon
  rind
1 tablespoon finely chopped fresh
  flat-leaf parsley
1 tablespoon finely chopped
  fresh basil
2 tablespoons finely grated
  parmesan cheese
vegetable oil, for shallow-frying
lemon wedges

green bean salad
125g fine green beans, trimmed
1 tablespoon lemon juice
2 teaspoons olive oil
2 tablespoons coarsely chopped
  fresh flat-leaf parsley

1 Using meat mallet, gently pound chicken, one piece at a time, between sheets of cling film until 5mm thick; cut each piece in half.
2 Whisk flour, egg and milk in shallow bowl; combine breadcrumbs, rind, herbs and cheese in another shallow bowl. Coat chicken pieces, one at a time, in egg mixture then breadcrumb mixture.
3 Heat oil in medium frying pan; shallow-fry chicken, until cooked. Drain on absorbent paper.
4 Meanwhile, make green bean salad; serve salad with chicken, and lemon wedges.

green bean salad Boil, steam or microwave beans until tender; drain. Toss beans in medium bowl with remaining ingredients.

prep + cook time 30 minutes
serves 2
nutritional count per serving
28.1g total fat (5.9g saturated fat); 2746kJ (657 cal); 38.5g carbohydrate; 59.9g protein; 4.6g fibre

CHICKEN WITH CAPERS, ANCHOVIES & ROSEMARY

2 teaspoons drained capers, rinsed, chopped finely
1 clove garlic, crushed
2 drained anchovies, chopped finely
1 teaspoon fresh rosemary leaves
2 chicken thighs (400g)

1 Combine capers, garlic, anchovies and rosemary in small bowl.
2 Preheat grill to hot.
3 Cut two deep slashes into each chicken thigh. Place a teaspoon of the caper mixture into each slash.
4 Cook chicken, skin-side down, under grill about 15 minutes; turn chicken, cook a further 15 minutes or until browned and cooked through.
5 Serve chicken with salad leaves and steamed baby potatoes, if desired.

prep + cook time 40 minutes
serves 1
nutritional count per serving
40.9g total fat (13.3g saturated fat); 2370kJ (567 cal); 0.9g carbohydrate; 49g protein; 0.6g fibre

TUNA & LEMON LINGUINE

100g linguine pasta
95g can tuna in oil
½ teaspoon finely grated lemon
rind
1 teaspoon lemon juice
1 tablespoon coarsely chopped
fresh flat-leaf parsley
1 clove garlic, crushed

1 Cook pasta in medium-sized saucepan of boiling water, uncovered, until just tender; drain.
2 Combine hot pasta with undrained tuna, lemon rind, juice, parsley and garlic in large bowl, toss gently.

prep + cook time 20 minutes
serves 2
nutritional count per serving
7.1g total fat (1.2g saturated fat); 1158kJ (277 cal); 34.4g carbohydrate; 17.4g protein; 2.1g fibre

MUSSELS WITH WHITE WINE & VEGETABLES

500g mussels
10g butter
½ small brown onion (40g),
   chopped finely
½ small carrot (35), chopped
   finely
½ trimmed celery stalk (50g),
   chopped finely
½ clove garlic, crushed
2 tablespoons dry white wine
2 slices crusty bread
1 teaspoon olive oil
2 tablespoons coarsely chopped
   fresh flat-leaf parsley

1 Scrub mussels; remove beards.
2 Heat butter in medium
saucepan, add onion, carrot,
celery and garlic; cook, stirring,
until onion is soft.
3 Add wine, bring to a boil. Add
mussels; cook, covered, about
5 minutes or until mussels open
(discard any that do not).
4 Meanwhile preheat grill.
5 Brush bread with oil; toast both
sides under grill until browned
lightly.
6 Sprinkle mussels and broth with
parsley; serve with toast, if desired.

prep + cook time 25 minutes
serves 1
nutritional count per serving
16.8g total fat (6.9g saturated fat);
1885kJ (451 cal); 46g carbohydrate;
20g protein; 5g fibre

GRIDDLED TUNA WITH CORIANDER DRESSING

150g tuna steak
125g baby new potatoes
2 teaspoons olive oil
2 teaspoons lime juice
½ small red onion (50g), sliced
  thinly
1 tablespoon pecans, toasted
50g baby spinach leaves

coriander dressing
½ teaspoon coriander seeds
1 clove garlic, peeled
3 tablespoons fresh coriander
  leaves
1 tablespoon olive oil
2 teaspoons lime juice

1 Using mortar and pestle (or blender or processor), pound ingredients for coriander dressing until smooth. Rub half the dressing over tuna; cover, refrigerate 30 minutes.
2 Meanwhile, boil, steam or microwave potatoes until tender; drain, slice thickly.
3 Cook tuna on heated, oiled griddle pan (or grill) until cooked as desired.
4 Combine remaining dressing with oil and juice.
5 Combine potato, onion, nuts and spinach; arrange on serving plate. Top with tuna; drizzle with dressing mixture.

prep + cook time 30 minutes + refrigeration time
serves 1
nutritional count per serving 43.5g total fat (7.8g saturated fat); 2767kJ (662 cal); 20.5g carbohydrate; 44.2g protein; 5.9g fibre
tips The tuna is best marinated an hour ahead. Recipe is best assembled just before serving.

CAJUN-STYLE BLACKENED FISH WITH GREEN RICE

150g basmati rice
20g butter
½ small green pepper (75g),
    chopped finely
375ml chicken stock
20g butter, melted
1 spring onion, chopped finely
1 tablespoon lemon juice
2 x 200g firm white fish steaks
2 teaspoons cajun spice mix
4 spring onions, sliced thinly
3 tablespoons finely chopped
    fresh flat-leaf parsley
½ teaspoon cracked black pepper

1 Place rice in sieve; rinse well under cold water, drain.
2 Meanwhile, heat butter in small saucepan; add pepper; cook, stirring, until softened.
3 Add rice and stock to pan; bring to a boil, stirring occasionally. Cover pan with a tight-fitting lid, reduce heat to as low as possible; cook rice about 12 minutes or until tender.
4 Meanwhile, combine melted butter, chopped onion and juice in small bowl. Brush half the butter mixture over fish; sprinkle with spice mix. Cook fish in small frying pan until blackened both sides and just cooked through.
5 Stir sliced onions, parsley and pepper into rice.
6 Serve fish with rice, remaining butter mixture, and lemon wedges, if desired.

prep + cook time 30 minutes
serves 2
nutritional count per serving
18.9g total fat (11.5g saturated fat); 2592kJ (620 cal); 63.1g carbohydrate; 47.7g protein; 1.9g fibre

GRIDDLED LAMB & PEPPER WITH OLIVE MASH

200g desiree potatoes, chopped
coarsely
2 tablespoons cream
10g butter, chopped
1 tablespoon coarsely chopped
black olives
½ small red pepper (75g),
quartered
2 lamb loin chops (200g)
2 tablespoons fresh mint leaves

1 Boil, steam or microwave potato until tender; drain. Mash potato with cream and butter in large bowl until smooth. Stir in olives; cover to keep warm.
2 Meanwhile, cook pepper and lamb on heated griddle pan (or grill) until pepper softens and lamb is cooked as desired.
3 Serve lamb with pepper and olive mash; sprinkle with mint.

prep + cook time 25 minutes
serves 1
nutritional count per serving
39g total fat (23.2g saturated fat); 2705kJ (647 cal); 32.7g carbohydrate; 38.8g protein; 4.6g fibre

FAJITAS WITH GUACAMOLE & SALSA CRUDA

1 clove garlic, crushed
1 tablespoon lemon juice
1 teaspoon ground cumin
2 teaspoons olive oil
300g lamb steaks cut into strips
1 small red pepper (150g), sliced thickly
1 small green pepper (150g), sliced thickly
1 small yellow pepper (150g), sliced thickly
1 small red onion (100g), sliced thickly
4 large tortilla wraps

guacamole
1 small avocado (200g)
1 tablespoon finely chopped fresh coriander
½ small white onion (40g), chopped finely
2 teaspoons lemon juice

salsa cruda
1 medium tomato (150g), deseeded, chopped finely
1 fresh small red chilli, chopped finely
3 tablespoons coarsely chopped fresh coriander
1 clove garlic, crushed
½ small white onion (40g), chopped finely
1 tablespoon lemon juice

1 Combine garlic, juice, cumin and oil in medium bowl; add lamb, stir to coat in mixture. Cover; refrigerate.
2 Meanwhile, make guacamole: place avocado in small bowl; mash roughly with fork. Add remaining ingredients, stir gently to combine.
3 Combine ingredients for salsa cruda in small bowl.
4 Cook lamb in heated oiled large frying pan, stirring, until browned all over and cooked as desired. Remove from pan; cover to keep warm.
5 Cook peppers and onion, in batches, in pan, stirring, until just softened.
6 Meanwhile, heat tortillas according to instructions on packet.
7 Return lamb and pepper mixture to pan; stir gently over medium heat until heated through. Divide fajita mixture between serving plates; serve with tortillas, guacamole and salsa cruda.

prep + cook time 45 minutes
serves 2
nutritional count per serving
40.6g total fat (11.1g saturated fat); 3382kJ (809 cal); 61.1g carbohydrate; 45.6g protein; 7.9g fibre

BEEF WITH ASPARAGUS & OYSTER SAUCE

1 tablespoon groundnut oil

250g beef rump steak, sliced thinly

1 small brown onion (80g), cut into wedges

170g asparagus, trimmed, cut into 2.5cm lengths

1 clove garlic, chopped finely

1 tablespoon oyster sauce

2 teaspoons japanese soy sauce

1 Heat half the oil in wok; stir-fry beef, in batches, until browned.

2 Heat remaining oil in wok; stir-fry onion until softened. Add asparagus; stir-fry until tender. Return beef to wok with garlic; stir-fry until fragrant. Add sauces; stir-fry until hot, season to taste. For extra heat, sprinkle with sliced fresh red chilli.

prep + cook time 25 minutes
serves 2
nutritional count per serving 15.1g total fat (3.8g saturated fat); 1166kJ (279 cal); 6.1g carbohydrate; 28.6g protein; 2g fibre
tips Try broccoli or tenderstem broccoli instead of the asparagus. Serve with steamed jasmine rice.

SPAGHETTI WITH PARSLEY BASIL PESTO

100g spaghetti
1 good handful fresh basil leaves
1 good handful fresh flat-leaf
  parsley leaves
2 tablespoons roasted pine nuts
2 cloves garlic, quartered
2 tablespoons finely grated
  pecorino cheese
80ml extra virgin olive oil
2 tablespoons finely grated
  pecorino cheese, extra

1 Cook spaghetti in medium saucepan of boiling water, uncovered, until just tender; drain.
2 Meanwhile, blend or process herbs, nuts, garlic and cheese until combined. With motor operating, gradually add oil in a thin stream until combined.
3 Combine spaghetti with a quarter of the pesto in medium saucepan; toss gently. Serve sprinkled with extra cheese.

prep + cook time 20 minutes
serves 1
nutritional count per serving
111g total fat (22.1g saturated fat); 5961kJ (1426 cal); 70.9g carbohydrate; 33.9g protein; 9.9g fibre
tip Store remaining pesto, in single portions, covered, in the freezer for up to two months.

PANCETTA & RADICCHIO RIGATONI

250g rigatoni pasta
3 slices pancetta (45g)
15g butter
1 small leek (200g), sliced thinly
125ml single cream
1 medium radicchio (200g), sliced thinly
3 tablespoons fresh flat-leaf parsley leaves
1 teaspoon finely grated lemon rind
2 tablespoons lemon juice

1 Cook pasta in medium-sized saucepan of boiling water, uncovered, until tender.
2 Meanwhile, cook pancetta in heated oiled medium frying pan until crisp; chop coarsely.
3 Melt butter in same frying pan; cook leek, stirring, until soft. Add cream; bring to a boil. Reduce heat; simmer, uncovered, 2 minutes.
4 Add leek mixture to drained pasta with half the pancetta and remaining ingredients; toss gently then sprinkle with remaining pancetta.

prep + cook time 25 minutes
serves 2
nutritional count per serving
34.4g total fat (21.3g saturated fat); 3252kJ (778 cal); 96.9g carbohydrate; 22g protein; 8.2g fibre

CHINESE OMELETTE

¼ small red pepper (30g), sliced
    thinly
1 spring onion, sliced thinly
20g bean sprouts
30g fresh shiitake mushrooms,
    sliced thinly
2 tablespoons fresh coriander
    leaves
3 eggs
2 teaspoons fish sauce
½ teaspoon oyster sauce
60ml vegetable oil
2 teaspoons oyster sauce, extra
¼ teaspoon sesame oil
chives, spring onions and extra
    coriander, to serve (optional)

1 Combine pepper, onion, bean sprouts, mushroom and coriander in small bowl.
2 Combine eggs and sauces in medium bowl; beat lightly. Add half the vegetable mixture to egg mixture.
3 Heat vegetable oil in wok, stirring to coat sides. When oil is just smoking, add egg mixture, then, working quickly using a slotted spoon or wok spatula, push the cooked egg mixture in from the sides of the wok (as for scrambled eggs) and the uncooked mixture to the outside.
4 When omelette is almost set, sprinkle remaining vegetables over one half of the omelette. Reduce heat to low; cook 1 minute, folding omelette in half over top of vegetables after 30 seconds. Remove omelette from wok with two lifters; drain on absorbent paper.
5 Combine extra oyster sauce and sesame oil in small bowl. If desired, top omelette with chives, extra coriander and spring onions. Serve omelette with oyster sauce mixture.

prep + cook time 25 minutes
serves 2
nutritional count per serving
36g total fat (6g saturated fat); 1603kJ (384 cal); 5g carbohydrate; 11.4g protein; 1g fibre

ASPARAGUS FRITTATA

cooking oil spray
1 small red onion (100g), thinly
  sliced
170g asparagus
2 eggs
2 egg whites
2 tablespoons low-fat cottage
  cheese
40g rocket leaves
2 tablespoons lemon juice
2 teaspoons baby capers, drained

1 Preheat grill.
2 Spray small ovenproof frying pan with cooking oil; cook onion over heat, stirring, 1 minute.
3 Cut asparagus into 2.5cm lengths. Add to pan; cook, stirring, 2 minutes.
4 Meanwhile, combine eggs, egg whites and cottage cheese in a medium jug. Pour over asparagus mixture in pan. Cook, uncovered, about 5 minutes or until frittata is browned underneath. Place pan under grill for about 5 minutes or until frittata is set.
5 Combine rocket, lemon juice and capers in small bowl; serve frittata with salad.

prep + cook time 25 minutes
serves 2
nutritional count per serving
6.3g total fat (1.8g saturated fat); 614kJ (147 cal); 5.4g carbohydrate; 16.3g protein; 1.9g fibre

SOMETHING
SPECIAL

GARLIC & CHILLI PRAWNS

300g uncooked king prawns
1 tablespoon extra virgin olive oil
1 clove garlic, sliced thinly
1 fresh small red chilli, deseeded, chopped finely
2 tablespoons coarsely chopped fresh flat-leaf parsley
½ teaspoon finely grated lemon rind

1 Shell and devein prawns, leaving tails intact. Cut along backs of prawns, taking care not to cut all the way through; flatten prawns slightly.

2 Heat oil in large frying pan, add prawns; cook until almost cooked through. Add garlic and chilli; cook about 2 minutes or until fragrant and prawns are just cooked through.

3 Remove from heat, stir in parsley and lemon rind.

4 Serve prawns with lemon wedges and crusty bread, if desired.

prep + cook time 18 minutes
serves 1
nutritional count per serving
19.2g total fat (2.7g saturated fat); 1258kJ (301 cal); 0.5g carbohydrate; 31.2g protein; 1.1g fibre

PROVENÇAL-STYLE FISH SOUP WITH GARLIC TOAST

400g can chopped tomatoes
100g char-grilled red pepper, chopped coarsely
1 tablespoon olive oil
1 clove garlic, crushed
¼ teaspoon fennel seeds
250ml fish stock
250ml water
150g firm white fish fillet, chopped coarsely
150g uncooked peeled prawns
1 tablespoon coarsely chopped fresh dill

garlic toast
2 thick slices crusty bread
1 clove garlic, halved
1 tablespoon olive oil

1 Blend or process undrained tomatoes with pepper until smooth.
2 Heat oil, garlic and seeds in medium saucepan over low heat, stirring, about 3 minutes or until fragrant.
3 Add tomato mixture, stock and the water; bring to a boil. Reduce heat, simmer, uncovered, 10 minutes.
4 Meanwhile, make garlic toast: rub bread with garlic, brush with olive oil. Cook in heated griddle pan until browned and crisp both sides.
5 Add fish and prawns to soup; simmer, uncovered, about 3 minutes or until fish is just cooked through.
6 Serve soup sprinkled with chopped fresh dill and accompanied with garlic toast.

prep + cook time 35 minutes
serves 2
nutritional count per serving
24.4g total fat (3.3g saturated fat); 2040kJ (488 cal); 27.6g carbohydrate; 37.3g protein; 4.1g fibre

GREEN CURRY WITH CHICKEN MEATBALLS

400g minced chicken
1 clove garlic, crushed
1cm piece fresh ginger (5g),
    grated
1 tablespoon finely chopped fresh
    coriander
1 tablespoon groundnut oil
1½ tablespoons green curry paste
375ml coconut cream
1 tablespoon fish sauce
1 tablespoon lime juice
2 teaspoons grated palm sugar
90g sugar snap peas, trimmed
40g bean sprouts
2 tablespoons fresh coriander
    leaves
50g roasted unsalted cashews
½ fresh long green chilli, sliced
    thinly

1 Combine chicken, garlic, ginger and chopped coriander in medium bowl; roll level tablespoons of mixture into balls.
2 Heat half the oil in medium frying pan; cook chicken balls until browned.
3 Meanwhile, heat remaining oil in medium saucepan; cook paste, stirring, about 1 minute or until fragrant. Add coconut cream, sauce, juice and sugar; bring to the boil. Reduce heat; simmer, uncovered, 15 minutes. Add balls to pan with peas; simmer, uncovered, until balls are cooked through and peas are tender.
4 Serve bowls of curry sprinkled with sprouts, coriander leaves, nuts and chilli.

prep + cook time 50 minutes
serves 2
nutritional count per serving
80.5g total fat (44.7g saturated fat); 4243kJ (1015 cal); 19.7g carbohydrate; 50.6g protein; 9.1g fibre

tip Palm sugar is available from some supermarkets and Asian food stores. If unavailable, use brown sugar.

SOY DUCK BREAST WITH NOODLES

1 duck breast fillet (150g)
1 tablespoon chinese cooking
  wine
1 tablespoon soy sauce
2 teaspoons finely grated fresh
  ginger
1 teaspoon white sugar
1 fresh small red chilli, deseeded,
  chopped finely
150g chinese broccoli, chopped
  coarsely
150g thin fresh egg or udon
  noodles

1 Score skin and fat of duck breast through to the flesh. Place duck in small bowl with combined wine, sauce, ginger, sugar and chilli. Cover, refrigerate 1 hour. Drain duck from marinade; reserve marinade.
2 Cook duck, skin-side down, in heated lightly oiled small frying pan, about 6 minutes or until skin is browned and crisp. Turn duck, cook 3 minutes or until cooked as desired. Cover duck, stand 5 minutes.
3 Meanwhile, boil, steam or microwave Chinese broccoli until just tender, drain.
4 Place reserved marinade in same pan; bring to a boil. Reduce heat, simmer, uncovered, 1 minute.
5 Place noodles in medium heatproof bowl, cover with boiling water; stand 2 minutes, separate noodles with fork. Drain noodles.
6 Serve duck with noodles and Chinese broccoli; drizzle with hot marinade.

prep + cook time 25 minutes + refrigeration time
serves 1
nutritional count per serving
17.5g total fat (6.9g saturated fat); 2098kJ (502 cal); 38.7g carbohydrate; 36.7g protein; 10.1g fibre
tips Duck breast can be marinated a day ahead. Store any leftover noodles, covered, in the refrigerator, for up to one week. If you can't get hold of chinese broccoli, you can use bok choy instead.

COCONUT FISH WITH CHIPS
& LEMON CORIANDER MAYO

500g floury potatoes
cooking oil spray
2 tablespoons desiccated coconut
25g stale breadcrumbs, toasted
1 teaspoon finely grated lemon
  rind
1 egg white
1 tablespoon skimmed milk
2 firm white fish fillets (360g)
2 tablespoons plain flour

lemon coriander mayo
75g light mayonnaise
2 teaspoons finely chopped fresh
  coriander
1 teaspoon finely grated lemon
  rind
2 teaspoons lemon juice

1 Preheat oven to 220°C/200°C fan-assisted.
2 Cut potatoes into 1cm-thick slices; cut slices into 1cm-thick chips. Place chips, in single layer, on baking parchment-lined oven tray; spray with cooking oil. Roast about 40 minutes or until browned and crisp.
3 Meanwhile, combine coconut, breadcrumbs and rind in shallow small bowl. Whisk egg white and milk in another shallow small bowl. Coat fish in flour; shake off excess. Dip fish in egg white mixture then coat in breadcrumb mixture. Place on prepared tray; spray with cooking oil. Cook for final 20 minutes of chips' cooking time.
4 To make lemon coriander mayonnaise, combine ingredients in small bowl until smooth. Serve mayonnaise with fish and chips.

prep + cook time 1 hour
serves 2
nutritional count per serving
12.9g total fat (5.1g saturated); 2186kJ (523 cal); 55.6g carbohydrate; 41.6g protein; 7.2g fibre

PRAWN & CHORIZO SKEWERS
WITH BEAN & TOMATO SALAD

12 uncooked medium king
  prawns (500g)
2 cloves garlic, crushed
1 tablespoon olive oil
90g green beans, trimmed,
  halved
2 medium plum tomatoes (150g),
  sliced
1 tablespoon pine nuts, toasted
1½ tablespoons coarsely
  chopped fresh flat-leaf parsley
4 x 20cm stalks fresh rosemary
1 chorizo sausage (170g), sliced
  thickly

lime mustard dressing
1 tablespoon olive oil
1 tablespoon lime juice
2 teaspoons wholegrain mustard
1 clove garlic, crushed

1 Shell and devein prawns, leaving tails intact. Combine prawns in medium bowl with garlic and oil. Cover; refrigerate 3 hours or overnight.

2 To make lime mustard dressing, combine ingredients in screw-top jar; shake well.

3 Meanwhile, boil, steam or microwave beans until just tender; drain. Rinse under cold water; drain. Combine beans in medium bowl with tomato, nuts, parsley and dressing.

4 Drain prawns, discard marinade. Remove leaves from bottom two-thirds of each rosemary stalk; thread prawns and chorizo, alternately, onto rosemary skewers. Cook skewers in heated oiled griddle pan until prawns are changed in colour and chorizo is browned.

prep + cook time 35 minutes + refrigeration
serves 2
nutritional count per serving
49.9g total fat (12.3g saturated fat); 2730kJ (653 cal); 5.4g carbohydrate; 45g protein; 3.4g fibre

SALT & SICHUAN PEPPER SALMON WITH WASABI MAYONNAISE

1 teaspoon sea salt
1 teaspoon sichuan pepper
1½ tablespoons vegetable oil
2 x 200g salmon fillets, skin on
75g mayonnaise
1 teaspoon wasabi paste
1 teaspoon finely chopped fresh
   coriander
1 teaspoon lime juice

1 Using pepper grinder or mortar and pestle, grind salt and pepper until fine. Combine pepper mixture, half the oil and fish in medium bowl, cover; stand 5 minutes.

2 Meanwhile, combine mayonnaise, wasabi, coriander and juice in small bowl.

3 Heat remaining oil in medium frying pan; cook fish, skin-side down, until skin crisps. Turn fish; cook, uncovered, until cooked as desired.

4 Serve fish with wasabi mayonnaise, together with watercress and a slice of lime, if desired.

prep + cook time 25 minutes
serves 2
nutritional count per serving
40.1g total fat (6.3g saturated fat); 2278kJ (545 cal); 7.5g carbohydrate; 39.4 protein; 0.2g fibre

HONEY DIJON LAMB RACKS WITH POTATO & SWEET POTATO GRATIN

1 tablespoon olive oil
1 teaspoon dijon mustard
2 tablespoons red wine vinegar
1 clove garlic, crushed
1 tablespoon honey
2 x 4 french-trimmed lamb cutlet racks (300g)
1 small sweet potato (250g)
2 small potatoes (240g)
2 teaspoons plain flour
180ml single cream, warmed
60ml milk, warmed
35g grated mozzarella cheese

1 Combine oil, mustard, vinegar, garlic and honey in large bowl; add lamb, turn to coat all over in marinade. Cover; refrigerate 3 hours or overnight.

2 Preheat oven to 200°C/180°C fan-assisted. Grease deep 1 litre ovenproof dish.

3 Using V-slicer, mandoline or sharp knife, cut sweet potato and potatoes into 2mm-thick slices; place half the sweet potato slices, overlapping slightly, in dish. Top with half the potato, overlapping slices slightly. Repeat layering with remaining sweet potato and potato.

4 Blend flour with a little of the cream in medium jug to form a smooth paste; stir in remaining cream and milk. Pour cream mixture over potato and sweet potato.

5 Cover gratin with foil; cook about 40 minutes or until vegetables are tender. Uncover gratin; sprinkle with cheese. Cook about 10 minutes or until cheese browns lightly. Stand gratin 5 minutes before serving.

6 Meanwhile, drain lamb; reserve marinade. Place lamb on wire rack in large shallow baking dish; cook, uncovered, in oven for the last 35 minutes of gratin cooking time or until cooked as desired. Cover to keep warm.

7 Bring reserved marinade to a boil in small saucepan. Reduce heat; simmer sauce, uncovered, 5 minutes. Serve gratin with lamb, drizzled with sauce.

prep + cook time 1 hour 40 minutes + refrigeration time
serves 2
nutritional count per serving
66.2g total fat (36.1g saturated fat); 3795kJ (908 cal); 49.2g carbohydrate; 28.4g protein; 4.3g fibre

LAMB CUTLETS WITH SALSA VERDE & PARSNIP PURÉE

1 large parsnip (350g), chopped coarsely
250ml chicken stock
2 tablespoons single cream
6 french-trimmed lamb cutlets (300g)

salsa verde
3 tablespoons coarsely chopped fresh flat-leaf parsley
3 tablespoons coarsely chopped fresh basil
3 tablespoons coarsely chopped fresh mint
1 spring onion, sliced thinly
2 tablespoons extra virgin olive oil
1 tablespoon lemon juice

1 Place parsnip and stock in medium saucepan; bring to a boil. Reduce heat, simmer, uncovered, 10 minutes or until parsnip is soft and stock is almost evaporated. Blend or process parsnip until smooth, return to pan; stir in cream, cover to keep warm.
2 Meanwhile, cook lamb on heated oiled griddle pan (or grill) until cooked as desired.
3 To make salsa verde, combine herbs, onion, oil and juice in small bowl.
4 Serve cutlets with salsa verde and parsnip purée.

prep + cook time 40 minutes
serves 2
nutritional count per serving
40.7g total fat (14.5g saturated fat); 2186kJ (523 cal); 17.6g carbohydrate; 20.3g protein; 4.9g fibre

FILLET STEAKS WITH ROASTED PARSNIP & BEETROOT

1 medium parsnip (250g),
  chopped coarsely
150g baby beetroot
2 tablespoons olive oil
1 clove garlic, crushed
1 teaspoon fresh rosemary leaves
100g cauliflower florets
150g asparagus, chopped
  coarsely
2 x 125g beef fillet steaks
20g parmesan cheese flakes

1 Preheat oven to 200°C/180°C fan-assisted.
2 Place parsnip and beetroot in small baking dish; toss with half the combined oil, garlic and rosemary. Roast, uncovered, 25 minutes.
3 Place cauliflower and asparagus on oven tray; toss with remaining oil mixture. Roast with the parsnip mixture, 20 minutes or until vegetables are browned and tender. When cool enough to handle, halve the beetroot.
4 Meanwhile, cook beef on heated, oiled griddle pan (or grill) until browned both sides and cooked as desired. Cover to keep warm.
5 Serve beef with vegetables; sprinkle with cheese.

prep + cook time 1 hour 5 minutes
serves 2
nutritional count per serving
29.5g total fat (7.8g saturated fat); 2098kJ (502 cal); 19.6g carbohydrate; 36.7g protein; 7.4g fibre

PORK CHOPS WITH APPLES & CALVADOS

2 x 280g pork loin chops
30g butter
1 medium apple (150g), peeled,
    cut into thin wedges
2 shallots (50g), sliced thinly
2 teaspoons plain flour
60ml calvados
125ml cider vinegar
125ml chicken stock
80ml single cream

1 Cook pork in heated oiled medium frying pan. Remove from pan; cover to keep warm. Drain and discard excess fat from pan.
2 Heat half the butter in pan; cook apple, stirring, until browned lightly. Remove from pan.
3 Heat remaining butter in pan; cook shallots, stirring, until soft. Add flour; cook, stirring, 1 minute. Add calvados; bring to the boil. Stir in cider, stock and cream; simmer, uncovered, until sauce thickens slightly. Return apples to pan; cook until heated through.
4 Serve pork topped with apple and sauce; serve with a green salad, if desired.

prep + cook time 30 minutes
serves 2
nutritional count per serving
47.5g total fat (25g saturated fat); 2947kJ (705 cal); 18.1g carbohydrate; 35.7g protein; 1.4g fibre

COOK & FREEZE

CREAMY PUMPKIN & POTATO SOUP

1 tablespoon olive oil
1 medium brown onion (150g),
  coarsely chopped
1 clove garlic, crushed
600g pumpkin, coarsely chopped
2 medium potatoes (400g),
  coarsely chopped
500ml water
375ml vegetable stock
60ml single cream
2 teaspoons lemon juice
garlic and herb croutons
1 tablespoon snipped chives

1 Heat olive oil in large saucepan; cook onion and garlic, stirring, until onion softens.
2 Add pumpkin, potatoes, water and stock; bring to the boil. Reduce heat; simmer, covered, about 20 minutes or until vegetables are tender. Stand for 10 minutes.
3 Blend or process soup, in batches, until smooth. Return soup to same pan; add cream and lemon juice. Reheat, stirring, without boiling, until hot. Serve bowls of soup topped with garlic and herb croutons and snipped chives.

prep + cook time 35 minutes
serves 2 + 2 servings to freeze
nutritional count per serving
29.3g total fat (11.7g saturated fat); 2006kJ (480 cal); 41.4g carbohydrate; 10.7g protein; 5g fibre

MEXICAN CHICKEN

2 tablespoons olive oil
1kg chicken boneless thighs,
    coarsely chopped
1 medium brown onion (150g),
    finely chopped
3 garlic cloves, crushed
800g canned chopped tomatoes
250ml chicken stock
60g jalapeño chillies, drained and
    sliced
420g canned kidney beans, rinsed
    and drained
fresh oregano leaves

1 Heat 1 tablespoon olive oil in large deep frying pan. Cook chicken, in batches, until browned. Remove from pan.

2 Heat remaining olive oil in same pan; cook onion and garlic, stirring, until onion softens. Return chicken to pan with tomatoes and stock; bring to the boil. Reduce heat; simmer, covered, about 25 minutes or until sauce thickens slightly.

3 Add chillies and kidney beans; stir until mixture is heated through. Serve sprinkled with oregano leaves.

prep + cook time 45 minutes
serves 2 + 2 servings to freeze
nutritional count per serving
28.3g total fat (7g saturated fat); 2345kJ (561 cal); 19g carbohydrate; 54.1g protein; 8.1g fibre

BEEF & ONION STEW

1kg braising steak, diced
50g plain flour
2 tablespoons olive oil
2 small brown onions (160g),
  coarsely chopped
2 cloves garlic, crushed
150g button mushrooms,
  quartered
250ml dry red wine
400g canned undrained
  tomatoes, crushed
500ml beef stock
2 tablespoons tomato paste

1 Coat beef in flour, shake away excess.
2 Heat oil 1 tablespoon olive oil in large saucepan; cook beef, in batches, until browned all over.
3 Heat remaining olive oil in same pan; cook onions, garlic and mushrooms, stirring, until onion softens.
4 Return beef to pan with wine, tomatoes, stock and tomato paste; bring to a boil. Reduce heat; simmer, covered, 40 minutes. Uncover; simmer about 40 minutes or until meat is tender and sauce thickens slightly, stirring occasionally.

prep + cook time 2 hours
serves 2 + 2 servings to freeze
nutritional count per serving
21.2g total fat (6.2g saturated fat); 2245kJ (537 cal); 17.4g carbohydrate; 56.8g protein; 4g fibre

CHILLI CON CARNE

2 tablespoons olive oil
750g braising steak, diced into
   2cm cubes
2 small brown onions (160g),
   chopped finely
2 cloves garlic, crushed
2 teaspoons ground cumin
1 teaspoon ground coriander
1 teaspoon chilli powder
1 tablespoon finely chopped fresh
   oregano
2 x 400g cans chopped tomatoes
125ml beef stock
2 teaspoons brown sugar
310g can red kidney beans,
   rinsed, drained

1 Heat half the oil in large saucepan; cook beef, in batches, until browned. Drain on absorbent paper.
2 Heat remaining oil in pan; cook onion, garlic, spices and oregano, stirring, until onion is soft.
3 Add undrained tomatoes, stock, sugar and beef; simmer, covered, about 1 hour or until beef is tender.
4 Stir beans into beef mixture; simmer 5 minutes or until heated through. Serve with crusty bread, if desired

prep + cook time 1 hour 55 minutes
serves 2 + 2 servings to freeze
nutritional count per serving
18.5g total fat (4.9g saturated fat); 1777kJ (425 cal); 17.2g carbohydrate; 43.9g protein; 6.6g fibre

MAPLE-GLAZED LAMB SHANKS

85ml maple syrup
250ml chicken stock
1 tablespoon dijon mustard
375ml orange juice
8 french-trimmed lamb shanks

1 Combine maple syrup, stock, mustard and orange juice in large deep flameproof casserole dish.
2 Add lamb shanks; toss lamb to coat in syrup mixture. Bring to the boil then cover tightly. Reduce heat; cook lamb, turning every 20 minutes, about 2 hours or until lamb is tender.
3 Serve with roasted potatoes and wilted baby spinach leaves, if desired.

prep + cook time 2 hours 15 minutes
serves 2 + 2 servings to freeze
nutritional count per serving
15.7g total fat (7.1g saturated fat); 2002kJ (479 cal); 25.7g carbohydrate; 58.9g protein; 0.3g fibre

SAUSAGES WITH BORLOTTI BEANS

1 tablespoon olive oil

8 thick Italian sausages

1 large brown onion (200g), chopped finely

3 cloves garlic, crushed

400g can chopped tomatoes

400g can borlotti beans, rinsed, drained

250ml beef stock

250ml water

2 tablespoons coarsely chopped fresh flat-leaf parsley

1 Heat the oil in large frying pan; cook sausages until well browned all over. Remove from pan; cool slightly then slice thickly.

2 Cook sausage pieces on cut surfaces until browned; remove from pan and drain on absorbent paper. Drain all but 1 tablespoon of the fat from the pan.

3 Cook onion and garlic in same pan until onion is soft. Add undrained tomatoes, beans, stock and the water. Return sausages to pan; simmer, uncovered, about 10 minutes or until mixture thickens slightly.

4 Sprinkle sausage mixture with parsley; serve with mashed potato, if desired.

prep + cook time 40 minutes
serves 2 + 2 servings to freeze
nutritional count per serving
51.1g total fat (22.8g saturated fat); 2884kJ (690 cal); 27g carbohydrate; 29.1g protein; 9.5g fibre

BEEF & RED WINE CASSEROLE

1.2kg braising steak, diced into
2cm cubes
2 tablespoons plain flour
2 tablespoons olive oil
400g pickling onions, halved
1 clove garlic, crushed
80ml dry red wine
580ml beef stock
1 tablespoon tomato paste
1 bay leaf
2 sprigs fresh thyme

1 Toss beef in flour; shake away excess. Heat oil in large saucepan; cook beef, in batches, until well browned.

2 Add onion and garlic to pan; cook, stirring, 5 minutes. Add wine; simmer, uncovered, until mixture is reduced by half. Add stock, tomato paste and beef; bring to a boil then reduce heat.

3 Add bay leaf and thyme; simmer, covered, 1 hour, stirring occasionally. Simmer, uncovered, for further 1 hour or until tender and thickened. Remove bay leaf and thyme.

4 Serve with mashed potato, if desired.

prep + cook time 2 hours 40 minutes
serves 2 + 4 servings to freeze
nutritional count per serving 15.4g total fat (4.8g saturated fat); 1471kJ (352 cal); 7.3g carbohydrate; 43.1g protein; 1.2g fibre

DESSERTS

STEAMED CHOCOLATE PUDDINGS WITH COFFEE ANGLAISE

60g butter, softened
75g caster sugar
1 egg
2 tablespoons finely chopped stale breadcrumbs
50g self-raising flour
1 tablespoon cocoa powder
1 tablespoon milk
2 tablespoons finely chopped dark eating chocolate

coffee anglaise
180ml milk
1 tablespoon caster sugar
2 egg yolks
2 teaspoons plain flour
2 teaspoons instant coffee granules
1 tablespoon boiling water

1 Grease two 180ml ovenproof dishes.
2 Beat butter, sugar and egg in small bowl with an electric mixer until just combined; stir in breadcrumbs, sifted flour and cocoa, milk and chocolate. Spoon into dishes. Top with a piece of baking parchment and foil, secure with rubber bands or string.
3 Place dishes in deep small frying pan; add enough boiling water to come halfway up the sides of dishes. Cover pan with tight-fitting lid; boil about 25 minutes or until cooked when tested with a skewer. Remove puddings from pan; stand 5 minutes.
4 Meanwhile, make coffee anglaise.
5 Dust puddings with extra sifted cocoa, if desired, and serve with coffee anglaise.

coffee anglaise Place milk in small saucepan; bring to a boil. Whisk sugar and egg yolks in medium bowl until creamy; add flour then slowly whisk in hot milk. Return mixture to pan. Stir over low heat, without boiling, until anglaise is thickened slightly. Dissolve coffee in the boiling water; stir into anglaise.

prep + cook time 45 minutes
serves 2
nutritional count per serving
41.9 total fat (25.3g saturated fat); 3227kJ (772 cal); 85.6g carbohydrate; 15.5g protein; 2.4g fibre

DATE & APRICOT CREAMY RICE

500ml milk
75g caster sugar
½ cinnamon stick
1 teaspoon finely grated lemon
    rind
50g uncooked arborio rice
30g dried apricots, coarsely
    chopped
60g fresh dates, coarsely
    chopped
1½ tablespoons coarsely
    chopped roasted unsalted
    pistachios

1 Combine milk, sugar, cinnamon and rind in small saucepan; bring to the boil. Gradually stir rice into boiling milk mixture. Reduce heat; simmer, covered, stirring occasionally, about 45 minutes or until rice is tender and liquid is almost absorbed.
2 Discard cinnamon stick; stir in apricots and dates, sprinkle with nuts.

prep + cook time 55 minutes
serves 2
nutritional count per serving
9.6g total fat (4.6g saturated fat); 1480kJ (354 cal); 56.5g carbohydrate; 8.6g protein; 2.4g fibre

INDIVIDUAL TIRAMISU

1 teaspoon granulated sugar
1½ teaspoons instant coffee
    granules
1 teaspoon cocoa powder, sifted
125ml boiling water
125g cream cheese, softened
160ml double cream
55g icing sugar
3 sponge-finger biscuits (45g)
1 teaspoon cocoa powder, extra

1 Blend granulated sugar, coffee and cocoa with the water in small bowl; cool.

2 Beat cheese in small bowl with electric mixer until smooth. Add cream and icing sugar; beat until smooth.

3 Halve biscuits crossways; dip in coffee mixture. Divide half the biscuits between two (310ml) glasses. Divide half the cream mixture between glasses; top with remaining biscuits then remaining cream mixture. Refrigerate 30 minutes. Serve dusted with sifted extra cocoa powder.

prep + cook time 20 minutes + refrigeration
serves 2
nutritional count per serving 49.5g total fat (31.8g saturated fat); 2805kJ (671 cal); 48.3g carbohydrate; 9g protein; 0.4g fibre

WALNUT & RICOTTA STUFFED FIGS

4 medium figs (240g)
1½ tablespoons walnuts, toasted
   and chopped coarsely
60g ricotta cheese
2 teaspoons caster sugar
2 tablespoons double cream
15g butter
2 tablespoons light brown sugar

1 Preheat oven to 200°C/180°C fan-assisted

2 Cut figs, from the top, into quarters, being careful not to cut all the way through; open slightly. Place on oven tray.

3 Combine nuts, cheese and sugar in small bowl; divide nut mixture among figs. Cook, uncovered, about 10 minutes or until figs are heated through.

4 Meanwhile, combine remaining ingredients in small saucepan; stir over heat until sugar dissolves.

5 Place two figs in each serving dish; drizzle with caramel sauce.

prep + cook time 15 minutes
serves 2
nutritional count per serving
22.8g total fat (12.2g saturated fat); 1526kJ (365 cal); 32.6g carbohydrate; 6g protein; 3.1g fibre

CARAMEL FONDUE WITH FRESH FRUIT

55g light brown sugar
80ml double cream
30g butter
125g strawberries, halved
1 medium banana (200g), sliced
   thickly
1 small pear (180g), sliced thinly

1 Combine sugar, cream and butter in small saucepan. Cook, stirring, until sugar dissolves and butter melts; bring to the boil.
2 Remove from heat; cool 5 minutes before serving with fruit.

prep + cook time 10 minutes
serves 2
nutritional count per serving
27.7g total fat (18.2g saturated fat); 2002kJ (479 cal); 52.8g carbohydrate; 3.3g protein; 4.6g fibre

PLUM TARTS

½ sheet ready-rolled puff pastry
1 egg yolk
1 tablespoon milk
4 small ripe plums (300g), sliced
    thinly
2 teaspoons caster sugar
½ teaspoon ground cinnamon

1 Preheat oven to 220°C/200°C fan-assisted. Line oven tray with baking parchment.
2 Cut pastry sheet in half, place each half on tray; brush with combined egg yolk and milk.
3 Overlap plum slices on pastry squares, leaving 2cm border. Sprinkle plums with combined sugar and cinnamon.
4 Bake about 15 minutes or until pastry is browned and crisp.

prep + cook time 25 minutes
serves 2
nutritional count per serving
12.4g total fat (6.1g saturated fat); 1058kJ (253 cal); 28.4g carbohydrate; 4.7g protein; 3.1g fibre

APPLE & BROWN SUGAR CRUMBLE

2 small apples (260g), coarsely chopped
2 teaspoons lemon juice
1 teaspoon brown sugar
¼ teaspoon mixed spice
2 tablespoons plain flour
20g butter, chopped
1 tablespoon brown sugar, extra

1 Preheat oven to 200°C/180°C fan-assisted. Lightly grease 250ml ovenproof dish; place on oven tray.
2 Combine apple, juice, sugar and half the mixed spice in medium bowl.
3 Place remaining mixed spice and flour in another medium bowl; rub in butter until combined. Add extra sugar; mix well.
4 Spoon apple mixture into dish; press crumble mixture over top of apples. Bake about 30 minutes or until browned.
5 Serve hot with ice-cream or cream, if desired.

prep + cook time 40 minutes
serves 1
nutritional count per serving
16.9g total fat (10.9g saturated fat); 1605kJ (384 cal); 54.4g carbohydrate; 3.3g protein; 4.5g fibre
tip We used Granny Smith apples in this recipe.

BAKED CARAMEL CUSTARD WITH ROASTED PEARS

55g caster sugar
1 tablespoon water
125ml double cream
60ml milk
1 egg
1 egg yolk
2 small pears (200g)
15g butter, chopped
1 tablespoon caster sugar, extra

1 Preheat oven to 160°/140°C fan-assisted.

2 Place sugar and the water in small saucepan; stir over low heat, without boiling, until sugar is dissolved. Bring to a boil; boil, uncovered, without stirring, until a golden caramel colour.

3 Remove from heat; gradually whisk in cream and milk. Return to heat to melt any undissolved caramel.

4 Beat egg and egg yolk in small bowl with whisk until combined; gradually whisk in cream mixture. Strain custard into medium jug.

5 Place two 125ml ovenproof dishes in medium baking dish. Pour custard into dishes. Pour enough boiling water into baking dish to come halfway up the sides of dishes. Bake, in oven, about 35 minutes or until custard is just set.

6 Remove custards from baking dish; increase oven temperature to 220°C/200°C fan-assisted.

7 Slice unpeeled pears lengthways. Place on medium greased oven tray. Dot with butter; sprinkle with half the extra sugar. Bake 15 minutes; turn pears over, sprinkle with remaining sugar, bake a further 15 minutes or until pears are browned and tender.

8 Serve caramel custards with roasted pears.

prep + cook time 1 hour 15 minutes
serves 2
nutritional count per serving 39.9g total fat (24.4g saturated fat); 2454kJ (587 cal); 52.7g carbohydrate; 7.4g protein; 1.8g fibre

HONEY GRILLED PLUMS & FIGS

2 small plums (150g), halved, stones removed
2 medium figs (140g), halved
1 tablespoon honey
2 teaspoons brown sugar
2 tablespoons thick Greek-style yogurt

1 Preheat grill.
2 Place plums and figs on shallow baking tray. Drizzle with half the honey, sprinkle with sugar. Place under grill until browned lightly and just tender.
3 Serve fruit, drizzled with remaining honey, pan juices and yogurt.

prep + cook time 13 minutes
serves 1
nutritional count per serving
3.4g total fat (1.9g saturated fat); 1104kJ (264 cal); 51.1g carbohydrate; 4.7g protein; 5.2g fibre

PEAR WITH COFFEE SYRUP

1 medium pear (125g)
2 tablespoons granulated sugar
125ml water
¼ teaspoon instant coffee
  granules
1 square dark eating chocolate
1 scoop vanilla ice-cream

1 Peel pear, cut in half crossways.
2 Combine sugar and the water in small saucepan; stir over medium heat until the sugar is dissolved. Add pear; simmer, covered, about 10 minutes or until pear is tender. Remove from syrup.
3 Add coffee to syrup; stir until dissolved. Serve pear with coffee syrup, chocolate and ice-cream.

prep + cook time 30 minutes
serves 1
nutritional count per serving
8.1g total fat (5.2g saturated fat); 1292kJ (309 cal); 57.7g carbohydrate; 2.7g protein; 2.8g fibre

BALSAMIC STRAWBERRIES
WITH CRÈME FRAÎCHE

125g strawberries, quartered
2 teaspoons balsamic vinegar
1 tablespoon icing sugar
1 tablespoon crème fraîche

1 Combine strawberries, vinegar and icing sugar in a bowl. Stand 30 minutes.
2 Serve strawberry mixture topped with crème fraîche.

prep time 10 minutes + standing time
serves 1
nutritional count per serving 8.1g total fat (5.3g saturated fat); 623kJ (149 cal); 15g carbohydrate; 2.6g protein; 2.8g fibre
tip Replace crème fraîche with yogurt or thick cream, if desired.

GLOSSARY

anchovies small, silvery, oily fish native to the Mediterranean; usually sold preserved in salt and packed in oil or brine. Anchovies have a strong flavour and should be used sparingly.

bok choy also known as pak choi, chinese white cabbage or chinese chard; has a fresh, mild mustard taste. Baby bok choy is much smaller and more tender than bok choy.

capers grey-green buds of a warm climate (usually Mediterranean) shrub, sold either dried and salted or pickled in brine. Rinse well before using.

cheese
brie soft-ripened cow's-milk cheese with a delicate, creamy texture and a rich, sweet taste. Best served at room temperature, brie should have a bloomy white rind and creamy, voluptuous centre which becomes runny with ripening.
cheddar the most common cow's milk cheese, cheddar ranges in colour from white to pale yellow, and has a slightly crumbly texture. A long maturing process gives

vintage cheddar a strong lingering flavour.
cottage fresh, white, unripened curd cheese with a lumpy consistency and mild flavour.
feta crumbly textured goat's- or sheep's-milk cheese with a sharp, salty taste.
haloumi firm, cream-coloured sheep's milk cheese matured in brine; can be grilled or fried, briefly, without breaking down.
mozzarella semi-soft cheese with a delicate, fresh taste; has a low melting point and stringy texture when hot.
parmesan also known as parmigiano; sharp-tasting, dry, grainy, hard cheese that originated in the Parma region of Italy. Made from skimmed or semi-skimmed cow's milk, the curd for this cheese is salted in brine for a month before being aged for up to 2 years.
pecorino generic name for hard Italian cheeses made from sheep's milk; if you can't find it, use parmesan.
ricotta soft, sweet, moist, white, cow's-milk cheese with a low fat

content (about 8.5 per cent) and a slightly grainy texture. The name roughly translates as 'cooked again' and refers to ricotta's manufacture from a whey that is itself a by-product of other cheese making.

chinese broccoli also known as gai lan and chinese kale; this vegetable is prized more for its stems than its coarse leaves.

chinese cooking wine also called shao hsing or chinese rice wine; made from fermented rice, wheat, sugar and salt with a 13.5 per cent alcohol content. Used for marinades and as a sauce ingredient, it can be purchased from most Asian food stores and some supermarkets; if you can't find it, replace with mirin or sherry.

chorizo sausage of Spanish origin; made of coarsely ground pork and highly seasoned with garlic and chillies.

fish sauce also known as nam pla or nuoc nam; made from pulverised salted fermented fish, mostly anchovies. Has a pungent smell and strong taste; use sparingly.

jalapeño chillies fairly hot green chillies. Available in brine bottled or fresh from specialty greengrocers.

japanese soy sauce made from fermented soy beans, Japanese soy sauce tends to be clearer and thinner than Chinese varieties with a sweeter, milder flavour. The recipe includes roasted wheat in and is brewed for many months.

maple syrup distilled from the sap of maple trees found only in Canada and parts of North America. Maple-flavoured syrup is not an adequate substitute for the real thing.

mustard

dijon pale brown, distinctively flavoured fairly mild French mustard.

wholegrain also known as seeded. A French-style coarse-grain mustard made from crushed mustard seeds and Dijon-style French mustard.

oyster sauce rich sauce made from oysters and their brine, salt, soy sauce and starches.

nuts as well as being a good source of fibre and healthy oils, nuts contain a range of vitamins, minerals and other beneficial plant components called phytochemicals.

cashews plump, kidney-shaped, golden-brown nuts with a distinctive sweet, buttery flavour and containing about 48 per cent fat. Because of this high fat content, they should be kept, sealed tightly, under refrigeration to avoid becoming rancid. We use roasted unsalted cashews in this book, unless otherwise stated; they're available from health-food stores and most supermarkets.

pecans native to the United States, these nuts are golden-brown, buttery and rich. Good in savoury and sweet dishes; especially good in salads.

walnuts a popular and versatile nut, the brown-skinned kernels have a ridged surface and are a source of antioxidants and beneficial omega-3 fatty acids.

palm sugar also called nam tan pip, jaggery, jawa or gula melaka; made from the sap of the sugar palm tree. Light brown to black in colour; usually sold in rock-hard cakes. If unavailable, use brown sugar. Available from some supermarkets and Asian food stores.

pancetta Italian salt-cured pork roll, usually cut from the belly; used, chopped, in cooked dishes to add flavours. Thin-cut bacon can be substituted.

pastrami spicy smoked beef, ready to eat when bought.

pea shoots the young, tender leaves of the traditional garden pea plant.

pine nuts also known as pignoli; small, cream-coloured kernels obtained from the cones of different varieties of pine trees.

radicchio leafy salad vegetable with dark burgundy leaves and strong, bitter taste.

rice

arborio small, round-grain rice; especially suitable for risottos.

basmati fragrant, long-grained white rice. Wash several times before cooking.

shiitake mushrooms cultivated fresh mushrooms with a rich, meaty flavour.

soy sauce made from fermented soy beans; several variations are available.

vinegar

balsamic authentic only from the province of Modena, Italy; made from a regional wine of white trebbiano grapes specially processed then aged in antique wooden casks to give the exquisite pungent flavour.

cider made from fermented apples.

wine based on fermented wine; red and white varieties are available.

wasabi Asian horseradish used to make the pungent, green-coloured paste traditionally served with Japanese raw fish dishes. Available from supermarkets and Asian food stores.

INDEX

anchovies: chicken with capers, anchovies & rosemary 37

apples
apple & brown sugar crumble 114
pork chops with apples & calvados 82

apricots: date & apricot creamy rice 105

asparagus
asparagus frittata 58
beef with asparagus & oyster sauce 50
beetroot, asparagus & feta salad 21
feta dip with asparagus, radishes & beans 13

avocadoes
fajitas with guacamole & salsa cruda 49
pork & cheese quesadillas with guacamole 25

bacon: egg & bacon salad 22

balsamic strawberries with crème fraîche 122

bananas: caramel fondue with fresh fruit 110

basil
lemon basil dressing 29
ricotta, basil & ham wrap 17
spaghetti with parsley basil pesto 53

beans (green)
feta dip with asparagus, radishes & beans 13
green bean salad 34
prawn & chorizo skewers with bean & tomato salad 73

beef
beef & onion stew 90
beef & red wine casserole 98
beef with asparagus & oyster sauce 50
chilli con carne 93
fillet steaks with roasted parsnip & beetroot 81

beetroot
beetroot, asparagus & feta salad 21
fillet steaks with roasted parsnip & beetroot 81

borlotti beans, sausages with 97

brie: ham, brie & fig salad 10

calvados, pork chops with apples & 82

capers: chicken with capers, anchovies & rosemary 37

caramel custard, baked with roasted pears 117

caramel fondue with fresh fruit 110

cheddar cheese
croque-monsieur 14
pastrami & cheese wrap 17
pork & cheese quesadillas with guacamole 25

chicken
chicken with capers, anchovies & rosemary 37
creamy chicken & pasta salad 18
dijon chicken & salad wrap 17
green curry with chicken meatballs 66
herbed chicken schnitzel 34
mexican chicken 89

chilli con carne 93

chocolate
pear with coffee syrup 121
steamed chocolate puddings with coffee anglaise 102

chorizo: prawn & chorizo skewers with bean & tomato salad 73

coconut fish with chips & lemon coriander mayo 70

coffee
individual tiramisu 106
pear with coffee syrup 121
steamed chocolate puddings with coffee anglaise 102

courgettes: ricotta, basil & ham wrap 17

cranberry sauce: turkey & cranberry wrap 17

crème fraîche, balsamic strawberries with 122

croque-monsieur 14

crumble, apple & brown sugar 114

curry: green curry with chicken meatballs 66

date & apricot creamy rice 105

dip, feta 13

dressings
coriander 42
lemon basil 29
lime mustard d73

duck: soy duck breast with noodles 69

eggs
asparagus frittata 58
chinese omelette 57
egg & bacon salad 22

fajitas with guacamole & salsa cruda 49

feta
beetroot, asparagus & feta salad 21
feta dip with asparagus, radishes & beans 13

figs
ham, brie & fig salad 10
honey grilled plums & figs 118
walnut & ricotta stuffed figs 109

fish
cajun-style blackened fish with green rice 45
coconut fish with chips & lemon coriander mayo 70
provençal-style fish soup with garlic toast 65
see also individual entries

fondue, caramel with fresh fruit 110

frittata, asparagus 58

garlic toast 65

green curry with chicken meatballs 66

guacamole 25, 49

haloumi: griddled vegetables & haloumi with lemon basil dressing 29

ham
croque-monsieur 14
ham, brie & fig salad 10
ricotta, basil & ham wrap 17

honey dijon lamb racks with potato & sweet potato gratin 77

honey grilled plums & figs 118

lamb
    fajitas with guacamole & salsa cruda
        49
    griddled lamb & pepper with olive
        mash 46
    honey dijon lamb racks with potato
        & sweet potato gratin 77
    lamb cutlets with salsa verde and
        parsnip purée 78
    maple-glazed lamb shanks 94
leeks: free-form caramelised leek tarts
    30
lemons
    lemon basil dressing 29??
    lemon coriander mayo 70
    tuna and lemon linguine 38
lime mustard dressing 73

maple-glazed lamb shanks 94
mayonnaise
    lemon coriander 70
    wasabi 74
mussels with white wine & vegetables
    41

noodles: soy duck breast with noodles
    69

olives: griddled lamb & pepper with
    olive mash 46
omelette, chinese 57
oyster sauce, beef with asparagus & 50

pancetta & radicchio rigatoni 54
parsley: spaghetti with parsley basil
    pesto 53
parsnips
    fillet steaks with roasted parsnip &
        beetroot 81
    lamb cutlets with salsa verde and
        parsnip purée 78
pasta
    creamy chicken & pasta salad 18
    pancetta & radicchio rigatoni 54
    spaghetti with parsley basil pesto 53
    tuna & lemon linguine 38
pastrami & cheese wrap 17
pears
    baked caramel custard with roasted
        pears 117
    caramel fondue with fresh fruit 110
    honey grilled plums & figs 118

pesto, spaghetti with parsley basil 53
plums
    honey grilled plums & figs 118
    plum tarts 113
pork
    pork & cheese quesadillas with
        guacamole 25
    pork chops with apples & calvados
        82
    sausages with borlotti beans 97
potatoes
    coconut fish with chips & lemon
        coriander mayo 70
    creamy pumpkin & potato soup 86
    griddled lamb & pepper with olive
        mash 46
    honey dijon lamb racks with potato
        & sweet potato gratin 77
prawns
    garlic & chilli 62
    prawn & chorizo skewers with bean &
        tomato salad 73
    provençal-style fish soup with garlic
        toast 65
pumpkin: creamy pumpkin & potato
    soup 86

quesadillas, pork & cheese 25

radicchio: pancetta & radicchio rigatoni
    54
radishes: feta dip with asparagus,
    radishes & beans 13
rice
    cajun-style blackened fish with green
        rice 45
    date & apricot creamy rice 105
ricotta
    mini baked ricotta with roast
        vegetables 26
    ricotta, basil & ham wrap 17
    walnut & ricotta stuffed figs 109
rigatoni, pancetta & radicchio 54

salads
    bean & tomato 73
    beetroot, asparagus & feta 21
    creamy chicken & pasta 18
    dijon chicken & salad wrap 17
    egg & bacon 22
    green bean 34
    ham, brie & fig 10

salmon, salt & sichuan pepper with
    wasabi mayonnaise 74
salsa
    cruda 49
    verde 78
salt & sichuan pepper salmon with
    wasabi mayonnaise 74
sausages with borlotti beans 97
sichuan pepper: salt & sichuan pepper
    salmon with wasabi mayonnaise 74
schnitzel, herbed chicken 34
seafood see fish; individual entries
soups
    creamy pumpkin & potato 86
    provençal-style fish 65
soy duck breast with noodles 69
spaghetti with parsley basil pesto 53
strawberries
    balsamic strawberries with crème
        fraîche 122
    caramel fondue with fresh fruit 110

tarts
    free-form caramelised leek 30
    plum 110
tiramisu, individual 106
tomatoes
    prawn & chorizo skewers with bean &
        tomato salad 73
    salsa cruda 49
tuna
    griddled tuna with coriander
        dressing 42
    tuna and lemon linguine 38
turkey & cranberry wrap 17

vegetables (mixed)
    griddled vegetables & haloumi with
        lemon basil dressing 29
    mini baked ricotta with roast
        vegetables 26
    mussels with white wine &
        vegetables 41

walnut & ricotta stuffed figs 109
wasabi mayonnaise, salt & sichuan
    pepper salmon with 74
wraps
    dijon chicken & salad 17
    pastrami & cheese 17
    ricotta, basil & ham 17
    turkey & cranberry 17

CONVERSION CHARTS

measures

One metric tablespoon holds 20ml; one metric teaspoon holds 5ml.

All cup and spoon measurements are level. The most accurate way of measuring dry ingredients is to weigh them. When measuring liquids, use a clear glass or plastic jug with metric markings.

We use large eggs with an average weight of 60g.

dry measures

METRIC	IMPERIAL
15g	½oz
30g	1oz
60g	2oz
90g	3oz
125g	4oz (¼lb)
155g	5oz
185g	6oz
220g	7oz
250g	8oz (½lb)
280g	9oz
315g	10oz
345g	11oz
375g	12oz (¾lb)
410g	13oz
440g	14oz
470g	15oz
500g	16oz (1lb)
750g	24oz (1½lb)
1kg	32oz (2lb)

liquid measures

METRIC	IMPERIAL
30ml	1 fluid oz
60ml	2 fluid oz
100ml	3 fluid oz
125ml	4 fluid oz
150ml	5 fluid oz
190ml	6 fluid oz
250ml	8 fluid oz
300ml	10 fluid oz
500ml	16 fluid oz
600ml	20 fluid oz
1000ml (1 litre)	32 fluid oz

length measures

3mm	⅛in
6mm	¼in
1cm	½in
2cm	¾in
2.5cm	1in
5cm	2in
6cm	2½in
8cm	3in
10cm	4in
13cm	5in
15cm	6in
18cm	7in
20cm	8in
23cm	9in
25cm	10in
28cm	11in
30cm	12in (1ft)

oven temperatures

These are fan-assisted temperatures. If you have a conventional oven (ie. not fan-assisted), increase temperatures by 10–20°.

	°C (CELSIUS)	°F (FAHRENHEIT)	GAS MARK
Very low	100	210	½
Low	130	260	1–2
Moderately low	140	280	3
Moderate	160	325	4–5
Moderately hot	180	350	6
Hot	200	400	7–8
Very hot	220	425	9